RIVERS OF INDIA

Yamuna the River with Playful Tales

SHUBHA VILAS

Om SHAKTI

An Imprint of **Om** Books International

Yamuna is worshipped as a Goddess who rides a tortoise, a symbol of creation. She was the daughter of Suryadeva Vivasvan, the Sun God.

She was especially attached to her twin brother Yamaraj, who was equally attached to his sister Yami.

River Yamuna is also called Kalindi because she begins her watery journey from the Kalinda Mountain who represents none other than the Sun god.
Yamuna then flows down and passes through another mountain known as *bandar punch* (tail of monkey).

Once Yamuna invited Yamaraj (the god of death) for lunch. She gave him a warm welcome and served him all his favourite dishes with utmost love and respect. She spoke sweet words that melted the heart of Yamaraj.

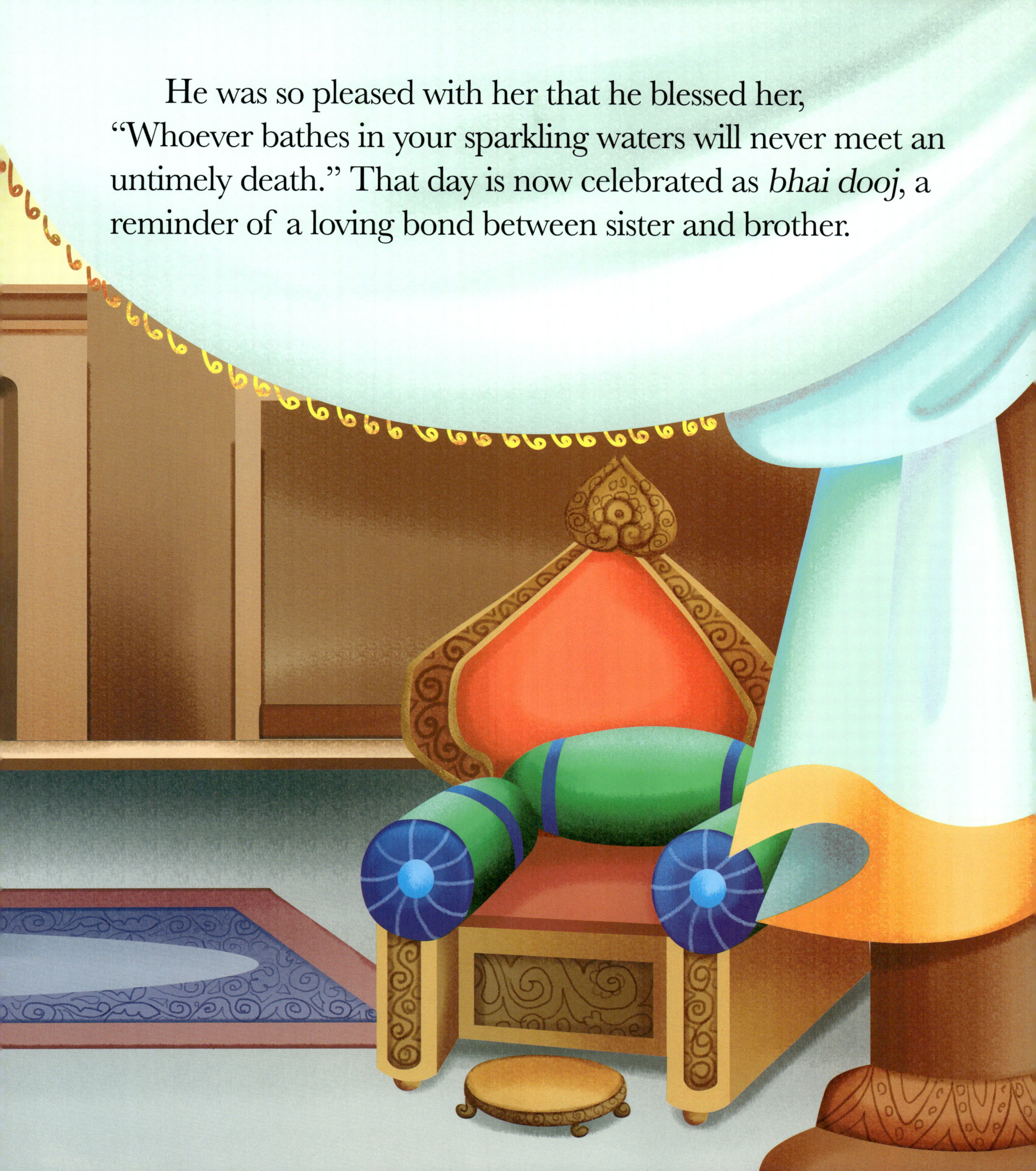

He was so pleased with her that he blessed her,
"Whoever bathes in your sparkling waters will never meet an
untimely death." That day is now celebrated as *bhai dooj*, a
reminder of a loving bond between sister and brother.

Once, the lovable and virtuous Hanuman, who had leapt across the ocean to reach Lanka in search of Mother Sita, wanted to cool down his tail after setting Lanka ablaze.

The salty ocean water would only worsen the burning on his tail. So Hanuman flew to the Yamuna, placed one foot on a mountain, and dipped his tail into the cool, refreshing river to soothe the heat.

At Yamunotri, Yamuna is joined by a small stream of Ganga, making it all the more auspicious. But why did Ganga need to come here?

Sage Asita had taken a vow that he would bathe in the holy rivers of Yamuna and Ganga every day. He had to travel a long distance to bathe in Ganga, but he did so every single day of his life. As he grew older, the arduous journey made it difficult for him to reach River Ganga.

He sent a heart-felt prayer to Goddess Ganga, "I have served you all life. Now that I am old and weak, I cannot come and take bath in your waters."
The compassionate Ganga understood his plight and said, "If you cannot come to me, I will surely come to you."

To help her devotee, Goddess Ganga took the form of a stream and merged into the River Yamuna at Yamunotri.

Yamunotri is a special place in the course of the Yamuna and a popular holy dham, of 'char dham yatra'. The chardham yatra begins with Yamunotri, followed by Gangotri, Kedarnath and ends at Badrinath.

Many of Lord Krishna's leelas took place on the banks of the River Yamuna. One such Leela was *Kalia Daman*. A poisonous snake Kalia had made River Yamuna his home and poisoned the Yamuna water. It was a big threat for the entire Vrindavan. Lord Krishna fearlessly danced on Kalia's thousand heads and destroyed his pride. Kalia then agreed to leave the River Yamuna and live far away.

When Lord Krishna told Radha that they would be appearing on Earth to perform their leelas, Radha grew worried. She asked, "How can we go without the presence of the Yamuna River?" Krishna gently assured her, "I have already sent Yamuna to Earth."

When Krishna appeared on Earth, the Yamuna became an integral part of many of his leelas, as he often played in its waters during his childhood. That is why the Yamuna shares the same dark blue complexion as Krishna. Simply by bathing in its waters, devotees receive the merit of visiting all holy places.